ATLAS OF WORLD FAITH

BUDDHISM

Anita Ganeri

W
FRANKLIN WATTS
LONDON•SYDNEY

First published in 2007 by Franklin Watts

© 2007 Arcturus Publishing Limited

Franklin Watts
338 Euston Road
London NW1 3BH

Franklin Watts Australia
Level 17/207 Kent St, Sydney, NSW 2000

Produced by Arcturus Publishing Limited,
26/27 Bickels Yard, 151–153 Bermondsey Street,
London SE1 3HA

The right of Anita Ganeri to be identified as the author
of this work has been asserted by her in accordance with
the Copyright, Designs and Patents Act 1988.

Series concept: Alex Woolf
Editor and picture researcher: Alex Woolf
Designer: Simon Borrough
Cartography: Encompass Graphics
Consultant: Douglas G Heming

Picture credits:
Art Archive: 13 (Musée Guimet Paris/Dagli Orti), 15.
Corbis: 4 (Michael Freeman), 6 (Lindsay Hebberd),
cover and 8 (Blaine Harrington III), 10 (Lindsay
Hebberd), 16 (Lindsay Hebberd), 19 (Christine
Osborne), 20 (Wolfgang Kaehler), 22 (Kevin R Morris),
24 (Pierre Colombel), 27 (Chris Lisle), 28 (Jose Fuste
Raga), 31 (Craig Lovell), 32 (Werner Forman), 34
(Galen Rowell), 36 (Chaiwat Subprasom/Reuters), 39
(Bettmann), 40 (Bojan Brecelj).

Every attempt has been made to clear copyright. Should
there be any inadvertent omission, please apply to the
publisher for rectification.

A CIP catalogue record for this book is available from
the British Library.

Dewey Decimal Classification Number: 294.3

ISBN: 978 0 7496 6979 9

Printed in China

Franklin Watts is a division of Hachette Children's Books.

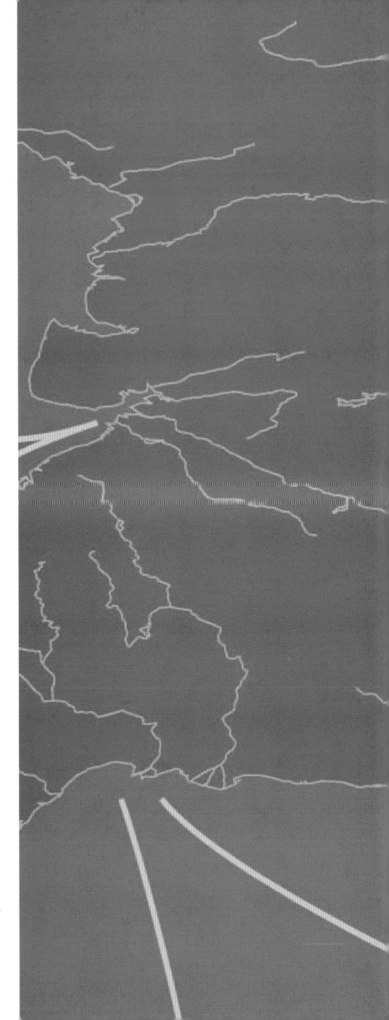

CONTENTS

CHAPTER 1:
THE LIFE OF THE BUDDHA

This stone carving from Cambodia shows the birth of Siddhartha Gautama, who later became the Buddha, in the garden in Lumbini, Nepal.

One of the world's major religions, Buddhism began in northern India some 2,500 years ago when a man called Siddhartha Gautama taught people a new way to live. He became known as the Buddha, or the 'Enlightened One', and his teachings were known as the Dharma. Since then, Buddhism has spread to countries all over the world, both in its Asian homeland and beyond. In each place, it has adapted to local traditions, merged with local beliefs, and faced many changes and challenges.

Birth of the Buddha The dates usually given for the life of Siddhartha Gautama are 563 to 483 BCE, although some scholars prefer 448 to 368 BCE. Legend says that he was the son of King Shuddhodana, the chief of the Shakya clan who lived in north-east India on the border with present-day Nepal. During her pregnancy, his mother, Queen Maya, dreamt that she was visited by a white elephant. This was a sign that the child she was carrying was destined to be a great person.

According to tradition, Siddhartha was born on the night of the full moon in May in a beautiful garden in Lumbini, Nepal. There are many stories to show that this was no ordinary birth. The gods showered the baby with flower petals, and a rumbling earthquake shook the Earth. Seven days later, Queen Maya died, and Siddhartha was brought up by his aunt in his father's luxurious palace.

A life of luxury Shortly after Siddhartha was born, a wise man called Asita came to the palace to visit

This map shows the main cities in northern India and Nepal at the time of Siddhartha's birth. Siddhartha grew up his father's palace in Kapilavastu.

the baby. Asita predicted Siddhartha's future. He told the king that his son would grow up either to be a great ruler or a great teacher, depending on what he discovered about suffering in life. Determined that Siddhartha should rule after him, the king tried to keep all knowledge of suffering from him. He kept Siddhartha safely inside his magnificent palace, sheltered from the outside world and surrounded by the finest things. As part of his education, Siddhartha learned the skills he would need to be a king and a warrior. These included archery, fencing and horse-riding. When he was 16, legend says, he married Yashodhara, a princess from a neighbouring kingdom. Following the custom of the time, he won her hand in an archery contest.

RELIGIONS IN INDIA

The period in which Siddhartha was born seems to have been a time of great religious change and upheaval in India. Old ideas were being challenged and debated, and new ideas were being put forward. At that time, the main religion in north-west India was Hinduism. Siddhartha may have been brought up as a Hindu, although no one is sure. Later, as the Buddha, he criticized the power of the upper-class Hindu priests and the formal nature of the Hindu religion, which seemed to exclude ordinary people. The Buddha taught that his path was open to everyone. It did not matter if people were rich or poor, what jobs they did, or which part of society they belonged to.

The Mahabodhi Temple in Bodh Gaya, India, where the Buddha gained enlightenment, is topped by a 50-metre high, pyramid-shaped spire. Inside the temple is a large, gilded image of the Buddha.

The Four Sights For many years, Siddhartha lived in great comfort. Under the king's careful supervision, he led a very sheltered life and never saw any kind of suffering. When he was 29 years old, however, he had an experience that changed his life. Disobeying his father's orders, he went for a chariot ride outside the walls of the palace. There he saw an old person, an ill person and a corpse. He had never seen such suffering before and was deeply shocked. Then he saw a wandering holy man. This man had given up his home and material possessions but still looked happy and contented.

Search for the truth Siddhartha decided to follow the holy man's example and to dedicate his life to searching for a way to end suffering. That night, he left home secretly, cut off his long hair and exchanged his fine clothes for rags. From then on, he would live as a wandering holy man with no money, belongings or home. Siddhartha spent some time with two religious teachers, learning how to meditate. Next, he spent six years living in the forest with a group of five holy men. They lived very hard lives, believing that this was the way to wisdom. Siddhartha underwent a series of terrible hardships (see panel) but they did not help him on his quest.

Enlightenment
Eventually, exhausted and weak, Siddhartha left his companions and made his way to the village of Bodh Gaya in north-east India. One evening, he sat down underneath a tall Bodhi tree to meditate, vowing not to move until he had discovered the truth. During the night, legend says, Siddhartha was visited by Mara, the 'evil one', who tried to tempt him away from his search. But nothing that Mara could say or do could disturb Siddhartha's resolve and, as the night drew on, he found the answers he had been looking for. Finally, he realized the truth about why people suffered and how he could help them. He had become the Buddha, 'the Enlightened One'.

GREAT HARDSHIPS

'I took food only once a day, or one in two or seven days. I lived on the roots and fruits of the forest, eating only those which fell of their own accord. I wore coarse clothes and rags from a rubbish heap. I became one who always stands and never sits. I made my bed on thorns. The dust and dirt of the years accumulated on my body. Because I ate so little, my limbs became like the knotted joints of withered creepers, my backbone stuck out like a row of beads and my ribs like the rafters of a tumble-down shed.'

(From the Maha-Saccaka Suttas)

This map shows the sites of the key events in the Buddha's life. He was born in Lumbini, gained enlightenment in Bodh Gaya, gave his first teaching in Sarnath and died in Kushinagara.

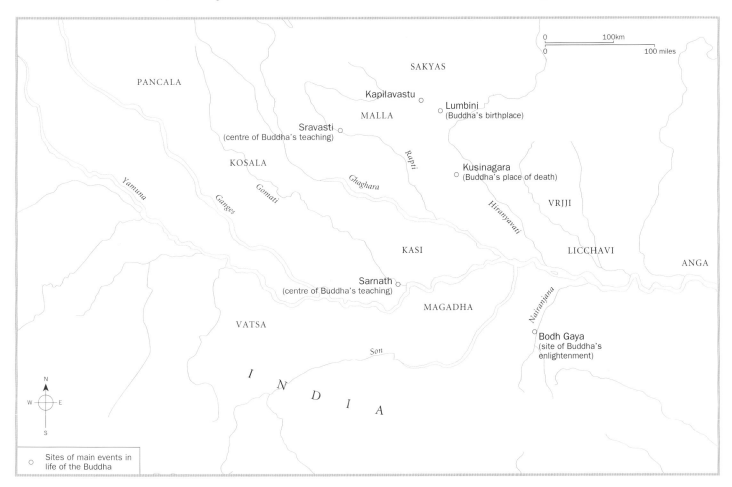

The first teaching After his enlightenment, the Buddha spent several days thinking over his experiences and continuing to meditate. He felt a deep sense of peace and joyfulness. During this time, he found his first followers – two passing merchants who brought him food. He then decided to teach his old meditation teachers (see page 6) what he had learned. On discovering they were dead, he next thought of the five holy men who had been his companions in the forest (see page 7). He found them in the Deer Park in Sarnath in northern India. To them, he gave his first teaching in which he explained the cause of suffering. This teaching is called the Four Noble Truths. The Buddha taught that everyone experiences suffering in life and that this suffering is caused by people not being content with what they have. There is, however, a way to end suffering, and this is by following the Noble Eightfold Path (see panel).

THE NOBLE EIGHTFOLD PATH

From experience, the Buddha knew that neither great luxury nor great hardship led to happiness. He taught a middle path, called the Noble Eightfold Path, between these two extremes. There are eight parts to the path:

1 Right understanding: understanding the truth of the Buddha's teaching.
2 Right intention: having compassion for other people and thinking about them in a kind and generous way.
3 Right speech: not telling lies, swearing or speaking unkindly.
4 Right action: not stealing, killing or performing any actions which might harm or upset other people.
5 Right livelihood: earning a living in a way that does not harm others.
6 Right effort: making an effort to be kind and compassionate.
7 Right mindfulness: being aware of your actions and thoughts.
8 Right concentration: training your mind to be calm and clear.

Many Buddhists have followed in the Buddha's footsteps and became monks like him. This young monk is studying the sacred texts in a monastery in Myanmar (Burma).

This map shows early Buddhist religious settlements in northern India. These were important centres for Buddhist teaching, both by the Buddha himself and the *sangha* of monks.

Establishing the *sangha*

The Buddha spent the next 45 years travelling around north-east India and teaching people from all walks of life. Many of his followers dedicated their lives to Buddhism. They became monks and nuns and were known as the *sangha*. (For some Buddhists, the *sangha* also includes laypeople.) During this time, the Buddha helped many other people to gain enlightenment as he had done. These people became *arahats*, or 'worthy ones' and were sent out by the Buddha to teach. Among them was the Buddha's own father. The Buddha's son, Rahula, was ordained as a monk.

The daily life of the Buddha and his monks and nuns is recorded in the Buddhist sacred texts. They possessed only a robe and an alms bowl. In the morning, they got up early and began their daily alms rounds, during which local people gave them food and other gifts. They ate their one meal at midday. In the afternoons and evenings, they listened to talks by the Buddha or another senior monk, then meditated long into the night. The *sangha* moved constantly from place to place, except during the rainy season when they took shelter in buildings, which became the first monasteries.

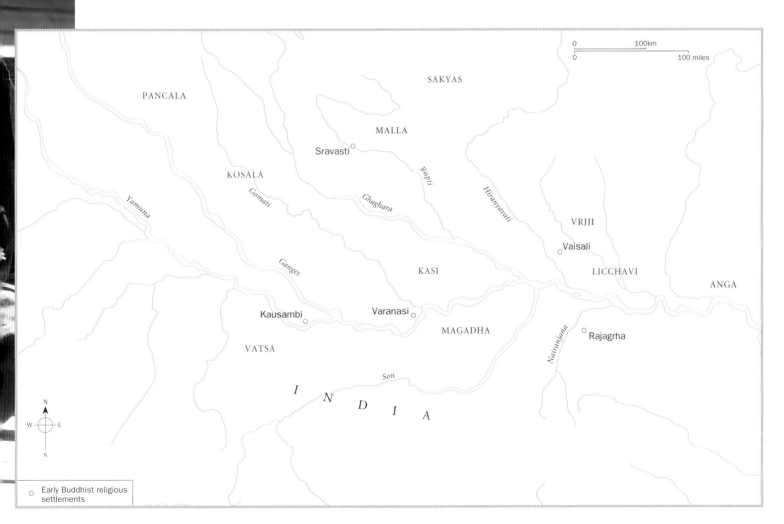

Early Buddhist religious settlements

Passing away

At the age of 80, the Buddha passed away. He had fallen ill with food poisoning and died in a grove of trees near the city of Kushinagara in northern India. Before he died, he told the monks not to be sad but reminded them of the teaching that everything changes and passes away. The Buddha did not name a successor but told the monks that his teachings should be their guide from now on. After the Buddha's death, the monks held a six-day ceremony in his honour, then his body was cremated. His ashes were divided into eight and given to eight different rulers. They built dome-shaped monuments, called stupas, over the relics.

The first Buddhist Council

The Buddha's teachings were not written down during his lifetime. Instead, they were memorized by his followers and passed on by word of mouth. According to tradition, shortly after the Buddha's death, a council of 500 monks was called at the village of Rajagrha in north-eastern India to agree on the content of the teachings. Two collections of teachings were recited from memory by two of the most senior monks, Upali and Ananda. It is believed that these two collections represented the authentic teachings of the Buddha. However, the collections were not written down for several centuries.

The second Buddhist Council

About 100 years after the first Buddhist Council, a second council was held in the city Vesali in north-eastern India. Over the years, differences in practice and teaching had begun to emerge. This was not really surprising as the *sangha* was not a single group but was

According to tradition, the Buddha was lying on his side when he passed away. This is called his parinirvana (passing into nirvana).

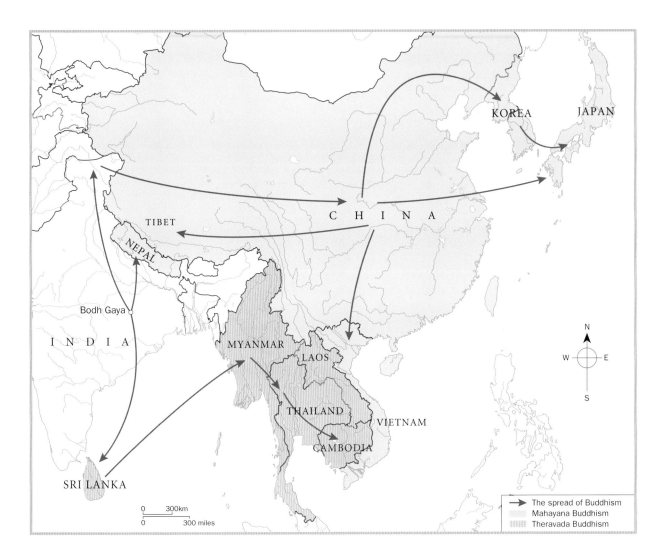

made up of many self-contained units with different schools of thought. The main dispute at the second council was about the sets of rules for how monks and nuns should live. Some groups of monks were following these rules less strictly than others – for example, by accepting money instead of gifts of food. Either at this council or some time later, this disagreement led the sangha to split into two groups: the Theravada, 'those who follow the way of the elders', and the Mahasanghika, 'the great assembly' and the forerunner of the Mahayana (see panel).

This map shows the spread of Buddhism outside India after the Buddha's death, and the countries in which Theravada and Mahayana Buddhism became established.

TWO GREAT SCHOOLS

Theravada Buddhists claim that the pure teachings of the Buddha, unchanged for centuries, are recorded in their scriptures called the Tipitaka. They believe that the Buddha was a human being, although a very special one. Mahayana Buddhists follow the teachings of the Buddha but also of other enlightened Buddhist teachers, and they have many additional sacred texts. They also worship mythical, god-like figures known as *bodhisattvas* who, out of compassion, choose to help other people to overcome suffering. From India, Theravada Buddhism spread south to Sri Lanka, Myanmar, Laos, Thailand and Cambodia. Mahayana Buddhism spread north to Tibet, China, Korea, Japan and Vietnam.

CHAPTER 2: EARLY BUDDHISM IN INDIA

In the centuries after the Buddha's death, Buddhism continued to develop both in India and beyond. The Buddha's followers spread the Buddha's teaching throughout India. Meanwhile, Buddhist missionaries were sent to other Asian countries where they established thriving Buddhist communities. At the same time, many foreign monks came to study at the great Buddhist universities of India. During this period, Buddhism became the main religion in much of India, often with the support of Indian and foreign kings.

The Greeks in India
In 336 BCE, Alexander (later Alexander the Great) came to the throne of Macedonia in north-eastern Greece. Within just 13 years he had conquered a vast empire, which stretched from Greece through Egypt and Persia, and into India. By 330 BCE, Alexander had defeated the Persian emperor, Darius. He now set out to reach the easternmost part of Darius's empire, the north-west of India. Alexander's armies reached India in 326 BCE. He defeated the Punjabi king, Porus, and his troop of 200 war elephants, at the Battle of Hydaspes. Alexander was so impressed by Porus's courage, however, that he left him in charge of the Punjab.

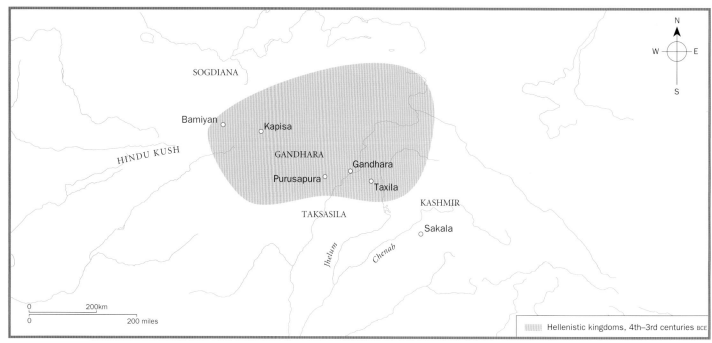

This map shows the location of the Hellenistic (Greek) kingdoms in India during the fourth and third centuries BCE, including the kingdom of Gandhara.

The kingdom of Gandhara

After Alexander's death, a Hellenistic (Greek) kingdom was established in the area around Gandhara, Purusapura and Taxila (see map on page 12). The kingdom became known as Gandhara. Buddhist missionaries were soon at work in the region, eventually gaining the support of local rulers such as King Milinda (see panel). Gandhara reached its height from the first to the fifth centuries CE under the Buddhist Kushan kings (see page 16). It also became the location of the first great Buddhist university, in Taxila, which attracted Buddhist scholars from far and wide and became a starting point for Buddhist missionaries travelling into Central Asia. Gandhara survived until the 11th century, when it was conquered by Muslim invaders.

Images of the Buddha

The first-ever images of the Buddha were produced by Gandharan craftsmen from around the first century CE. Before this, the Buddha had not been shown in person but by symbols such as an empty throne, a stupa, a Bodhi tree, a footprint or an animal. The style of these early images was very strongly influenced by Greek art. In Gandharan art, Indian and Greek sculpture mixed to produce graceful statues draped in long, flowing robes. From India, traders passing through Gandhara carried Gandharan art into Central Asia and China.

This standing Buddha from Gandhara shows the mixture of Indian and Greek styles.

MILINDA'S QUESTIONS

Many of the Greek rulers were influenced by Buddhism, including King Milinda (ruled 155–130 BCE). (*Milinda* is the Indian version of the Greek name, Menandros.) Milinda is said to have had a famous debate about Buddhism with the great teacher and monk, Nagasena. The king asked Nagasena a series of questions about the Buddha's teaching. Afterwards, it is said, he was so impressed that he converted to Buddhism. The debate is recorded in an important Buddhist text called 'The Questions of King Milinda'.

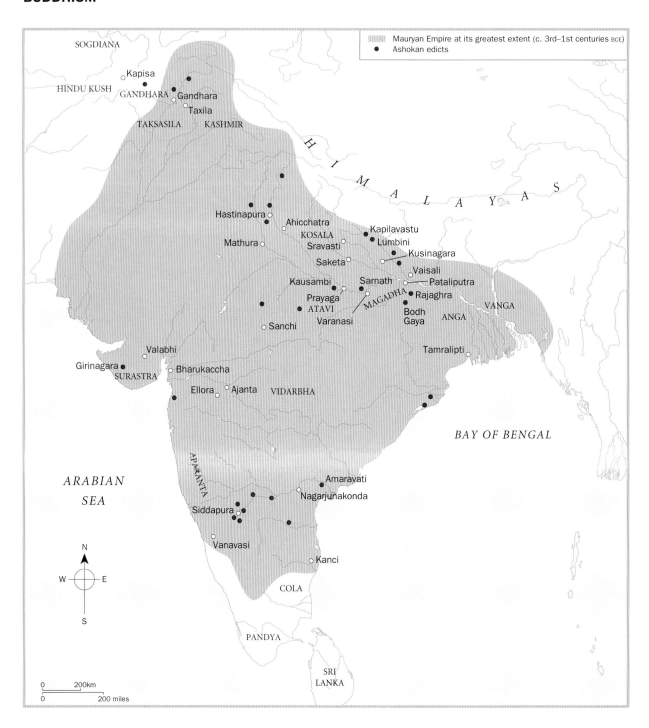

This map shows the Mauryan Empire under Ashoka.

The Mauryan Empire In about 321 BCE, Chandragupta Maurya conquered the area of northern India where the Buddha had taught, and founded the great Mauryan Empire. Chandragupta established his capital at Pataliputra (the modern-day city of Patna). Under his grandson Ashoka (ruled 265–232 BCE), the empire reached its greatest extent. Soon, most of India, apart from the extreme south, had come under Mauryan rule, but at the cost of thousands of lives. In about 260 BCE, Ashoka launched a particularly ruthless campaign against the region of Kalinga on the east coast. It was one of the few places in India to resist the Mauryans. According to some accounts, 100,000 people were killed in the battle and thousands more were injured or taken prisoner. Afterwards, Ashoka was filled with remorse. To make amends, he converted to Buddhism, with its teaching of non-violence.

Ashoka and Buddhism Ashoka became the greatest patron and supporter of Buddhism in ancient India. During his rule, all the existing Buddhist centres were greatly expanded, and new monasteries and stupas were built. More importantly, Ashoka vowed to establish a society based not on war and violence but on the Buddhist principles of compassion and peace. He himself tried to set an example. He travelled widely through the empire listening to people's opinions about what would make their lives easier. In response, he built much-needed wells and reservoirs, set up free hospitals for the poor, planted trees and provided welfare services for prisoners. He gave up hunting, his favourite sport, and instead went on pilgrimages to holy places linked with the Buddha's life. He also sent missionaries out of India to spread the Buddha's teaching.

Ashoka's edicts

Throughout his empire, Ashoka had a series of edicts carved onto rock faces and sandstone pillars. These were written in the ancient Indian language of Magadhi and were deciphered for the first time in 1837 by British scholar James Prinsep. They were placed at the borders of the empire and in places connected with the Buddha. Some edicts told of Ashoka's conversion to Buddhism. Others explained the Buddha's teachings and told people to behave accordingly, by living responsible and moral lives, helping others, being generous and truthful, and not killing or harming living beings. Special officers were also appointed to travel through the empire explaining the Buddha's teachings.

LION CAPITAL

The famous lion capital once stood on top of one of Ashoka's finest pillars. It was located in the Deer Park at Sarnath where the Buddha gave his first talk. The four lions face in four different directions to show that the Buddha's teachings reach all four corners of the Earth. Below are four royal animals – the horse, bull, lion and elephant – and four wheels, which represent the Buddha's teachings. The lions orginally supported a huge wheel, a symbol of Buddhism. Today, the lion capital is the state symbol of modern India.

Ashoka's lion capital is now in the museum at Sarnath.

The Kushan Empire

After Ashoka's death in 231 BCE, the Mauryan Empire began to break up. The empire finally collapsed in 184 BCE. After a period of unrest, India was invaded by the Scythian people from Central Asia, who founded the Kushan Empire. Their king, Kanishka (78–102 CE), was a keen supporter of Buddhism and, in about 100 CE, called Buddhists together for a Fourth Council in Kashmir. (Ashoka had ordered the Third Council in about 250 BCE in Pataliputra.) Since the collapse of the Mauryan Empire, Buddhism had split into 18 different schools. The aim of the Fourth Council was to try to bring these different schools together and to approve a new set of scriptures, written in Sanskrit, the ancient religious language of India. These scriptures became associated with the Mahayana school.

The rise of the Guptas

With the decline of the Kushan Empire, Chandra Gupta I (320–c. 330 CE) established the Gupta Empire across northern India. Under the Guptas, a golden age of Indian culture and history began. Literature, art and religion flourished, and even though the Guptas largely followed the Hindu religion, Buddhism was still given royal support. Great Buddhist universities were established at Nalanda (see panel) and in other locations. New Buddhist texts were written, and many fine works of art were created, including the paintings inside the Buddhist cave temples at Ajanta in western India, which can still be seen today. The Gupta Empire lasted until the sixth century CE when it was attacked by the Huns, a people from Central Asia.

Buddhism declines

The Huns destroyed many Buddhist centres in north-west India, including Taxila (see page 13). Over the next few centuries, Buddhism survived but no longer enjoyed

NALANDA UNIVERSITY

The greatest university in the Buddhist world was at Nalanda (in modern Bihar). It may already have existed in the Buddha's lifetime. In its heyday in the fifth century CE, it attracted over 10,000 students and 1,500 teachers from all over India and Asia. Subjects included the study of the Buddhist scriptures, Hinduism, philosophy, astronomy, mathematics and medicine. Among Nalanda's most famous teachers was the monk Nagarjuna (c. second century CE), who founded the influential Madhyamaka (Middle Path) school of Mahayana Buddhism. His main teaching was on the Buddhist concept of *sunyata* (emptiness), the idea that nothing has an individual soul or self.

The ruins of the great Buddhist university of Nalanda in Bihar, India.

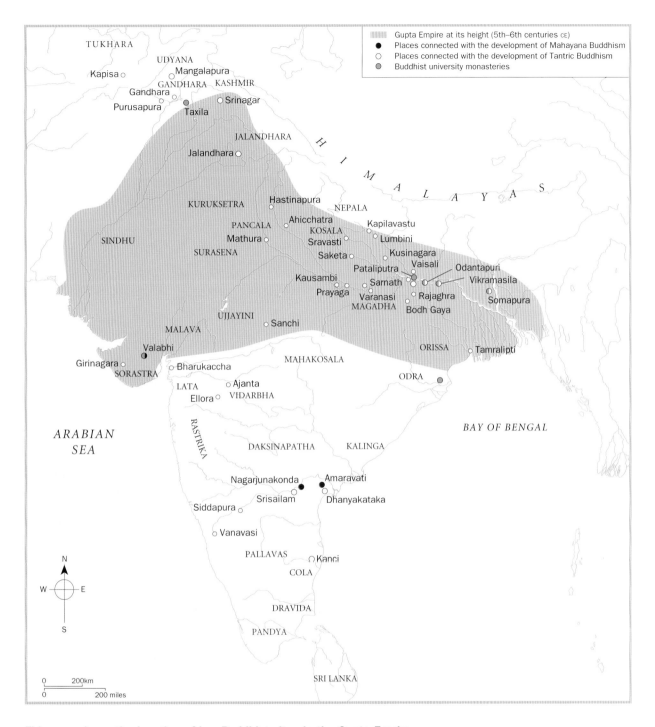

Legend:
- Gupta Empire at its height (5th–6th centuries CE)
- ● Places connected with the development of Mahayana Buddhism
- ○ Places connected with the development of Tantric Buddhism
- ● Buddhist university monasteries

This map shows the location of key Buddhist sites in the Gupta Empire.

royal support. But it was the series of devastating raids by Muslims from Afghanistan from the 11th century onwards that finally ended 1,700 years of Buddhism in India. The peace-loving nature of Buddhism made it an easy target for the Muslim armies. Monasteries were destroyed, and, in 1199, Nalanda was burned to the ground and its monks slaughtered. Since then, Buddhism has never really recovered in India, and Hinduism remains the country's major religion. India still attracts Buddhist pilgrims from all over the world to visit its sacred sites, but as recently as 1991, only 1 percent of Indians counted themselves as Buddhist. (See panel on page 36 for more about modern Buddhism in India.)

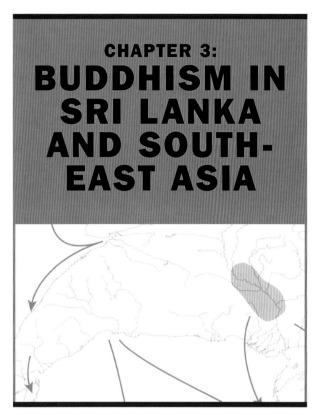

CHAPTER 3:
BUDDHISM IN SRI LANKA AND SOUTH-EAST ASIA

Ashoka's reign (see pages 14–15) was a crucial time for the expansion of Buddhism. From India, Ashoka sent out missionary monks to spread the Buddha's teachings. The first country outside India to which Buddhism spread was the island of Sri Lanka, off the southern coast of India, where it quickly became the major religion. Buddhism later spread throughout South-East Asia, including Indonesia, Myanmar, Vietnam, Cambodia, Laos and Thailand.

Buddhism reaches Sri Lanka

Buddhism was introduced to Sri Lanka in about 250 BCE by missionaries sent by Ashoka. They were supposedly led by Ashoka's own son, Mahinda, who had become a Buddhist monk. He converted King Tissa to Buddhism. Later, Ashoka's daughter, the nun Sanghamitta, visited the island and brought a cutting of the original Bodhi tree, under which the Buddha gained enlightenment. It was planted in the capital city of Anuradhapura, where it still grows today.

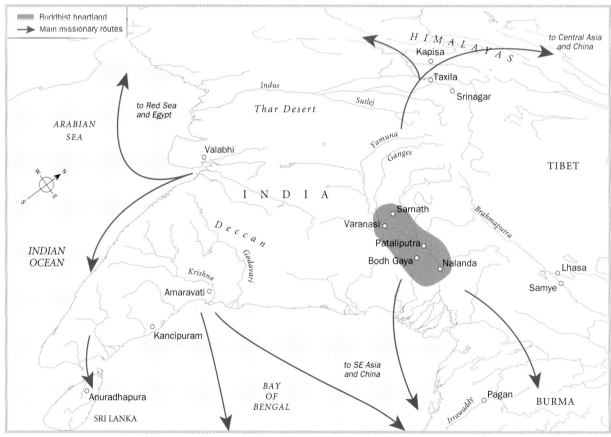

This map shows the main routes taken by the first Buddhist missionaries outside India.

During the second century BCE, Tamil invaders from India ruled parts of Sri Lanka, and Buddhism suffered. Many monks fled or died. At about this time, the Tipitaka was written down for fear of it being lost, because there were not enough monks to remember it.

RIVAL MONASTERIES

At Anuradhapura, King Tissa built the Mahavihara (Great Monastery) for Mahinda and his monks. The Mahavihara became the headquarters of Theravada Buddhism. In the first century BCE, however, the monks' position was threatened when another great monastery, the Abhayagiri, was built. The Abhayagiri became associated with Mahayana Buddhism, and a fierce rivalry began between the two monasteries. Mahayana Buddhism did not achieve a lasting hold in Sri Lanka, however, and by the 12th century the Abhayagiri had declined. Sri Lanka became, and remains, a Theravada country.

Buddhism falls and rises Between the first and seventh centuries CE, Buddhism thrived in Sri Lanka. From the seventh to twelfth centuries, however, South Indian kings invaded the island, and Buddhism declined. In 1070, King Vijayabahu (ruled 1055–1110) recaptured the island and set about restoring Buddhism. But it was in such a poor state that he had to bring an order of monks from Myanmar to form a new *sangha*. In the 12th century, King Parakramabahu (ruled 1153–1186) defeated the Indians and built many magnificent monasteries and stupas in the new capital of Polonnaruwa. With the arrival of Europeans on the island in the 16th and 17th centuries, Buddhism suffered as the Europeans tried to convert the islanders to Christianity. But there was another revival in the 18th century when several new orders of monks were formed. From 1796 to 1948, Sri Lanka was part of the British Empire, attracting followers who helped to spread Buddhism to the West (see pages 38–41).

Buddhism today After more than 2,300 years, Sri Lanka remains a proudly Buddhist country and the homeland of the Theravada tradition. Some 80 percent of the islanders are Sinhalese, most of whom are Buddhists. With some 15,000 monks, the sangha remains at the centre of Buddhist life, and the monks are held in great respect by the community.

A Buddhist shrine at Mihintale, Sri Lanka, where Mahinda met the island's king.

An image of the seated Buddha next to a stupa on the upper terrace at Borobodur. The monument has over 400 Buddha images.

Buddhism in Indonesia According to tradition, the first Buddhists to reach South-East Asia were missionaries sent by Ashoka in the third century BCE. They travelled along sea trade routes to the 'Land of Gold' – probably the west coast of Indonesia. But Buddhism really began to make an impact in Indonesia in the first century CE, by which time many Indians had settled in the region.

Buddhist kingdoms Between about 600 and 800 CE, the mainly Buddhist kingdom of Srivijaya ruled Sumatra. By the seventh century, there were Theravada communities in Srivijaya, with Mahayana arriving shortly afterwards. The great Indian Buddhist teacher, Atisha, studied in Srivijaya in the 12th century, and students travelled from Indonesia to study at Nalanda University. Indonesia was also a regular stopping point for Chinese Buddhist monks on their way to India.

In Java, both Buddhism and Hinduism were followed, with Buddhism becoming the dominant religion. In the eighth century, the Shailendra kings came to power and were strong patrons of Mahayana Buddhism. Their capital at Palembang became a great centre of Buddhist learning. In around 800 CE, the Shailendras sponsored the building of Borobodur (see panel).

BOROBODUR

The astonishing Buddhist monument of Borobodur was built on a hill, in the form of a gigantic stepped pyramid, six storeys tall. A stupa stands on the summit. Below this are three circular terraces representing the stages towards enlightenment in a person's life. The whole monument is shaped like a lotus flower, a sacred symbol of Buddhism. Each terrace is decorated with images of the Buddha and with scenes from his life. When Buddhism declined in Indonesia, Borobodur was abandoned. It was only rediscovered in 1814.

Buddhism in Myanmar Buddhism did not become well established in Myanmar until the Mon period, from the fifth to the tenth centuries CE. The Mon people of southern Myanmar followed the Theravada tradition, as did the Pyu people of central Myanmar. Mahayana Buddhism may have arrived earlier than Theravada, but did not take hold. In the 11th century, King Anuruddha (1044–1077) overthrew the Mon and unified the country. During his rule, Theravada Buddhism became firmly established. Anuruddha built his capital at Pagan, which is still famous for its amazing Buddhist ruins. Myanmar was later invaded by the Thais, who adopted Theravada Buddhism (see page 22).

This map shows the spread of Theravada and Mahayana Buddhism into South-East Asia from the first century BCE.

In 1886, the country became part of the British Empire. For many people in Myanmar, Buddhism became a powerful symbol of national identity during the periods when they were ruled by foreign powers.

Buddhism today From the 13th century, Islam became the major religion of Indonesia, although a mixture of Buddhism and Hinduism still survives in Bali and in parts of Java. In the 20th century, Buddhism enjoyed a revival and there are now about three million Buddhists in Indonesia.

In Myanmar, Buddhism remains the national religion, practised by about 85 percent of the population. Despite the country's harsh military government, Buddhism continues to thrive, with thousands of monks and nuns, and some 6,000 monasteries.

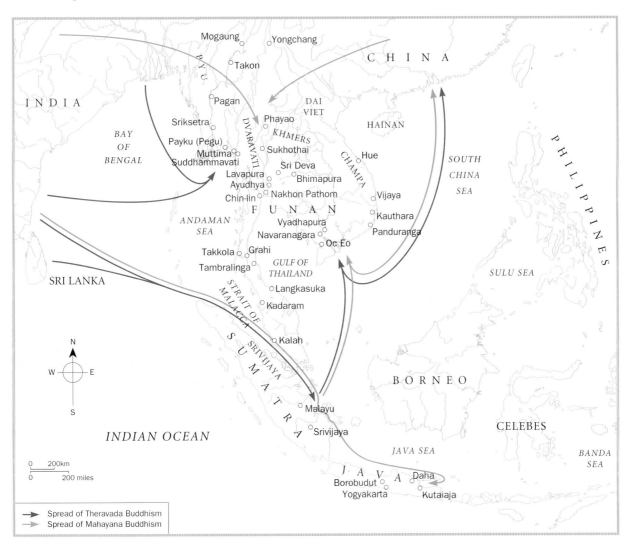

A young monk in Thailand collects alms from a Thai Buddhist outside a monastery. Buddhism remains very strong in Thailand.

Buddhism in Vietnam

Theravada missionaries may have reached Vietnam by sea as early as the second century CE, but the story of Buddhism in Vietnam really begins in 580 CE. An Indian monk, Vinitaruci, who had studied in China, arrived in Vietnam and brought Mahayana Buddhism with him. Mahayana quickly took hold in Vietnam and when the country was unified in 939 CE, it became the national religion. Two schools of Chinese Mahayana Buddhism – Chan (Zen) and Pure Land – became particularly popular. Buddhism was well supported by the Vietnamese kings, who regularly appointed monks to key positions at court. Over the following centuries, Buddhism became closely linked with Vietnamese nationalism. From 1883 to 1954, Vietnam came under French rule. Two Buddhist movements played a part in the struggle for independence: the Central Vietnamese Buddhist Association and the General Association of Buddhism in Vietnam.

Buddhism in Cambodia and Laos

In the ninth century CE, Cambodia had strong links with both India and China, but its Khmer rulers preferred Hinduism to Buddhism. Influenced by the Shailendra kings of Java, the Cambodian kings began to build 'temple mountains' like Borobodur (see page 20), the greatest of which was called Angkor Wat. But, unlike Buddhist Borobodur, their monuments were Hindu. This changed, however, with the reign of King Jayavarman VII (ruled 1181–c. 1215). He converted to Mahayana Buddhism, and the country became Buddhist. From the early 13th century, Cambodia experienced a series of invasions by the Thais. And thereafter, possibly under the influence of the invaders, the kings of Cambodia became Theravada Buddhists.

During this time, the neighbouring country of Laos fell under the control of the Khmer, the Thais and Myanmar. When Laos regained its independence in 1350, Theravada Buddhism was introduced, and the king invited monks from Cambodia and Sri Lanka to his court to act as his advisors.

Buddhism in Thailand

The Thai kingdom of Sukhothai, which lasted from the early 12th century to 1350, adopted Theravada Buddhism from the people

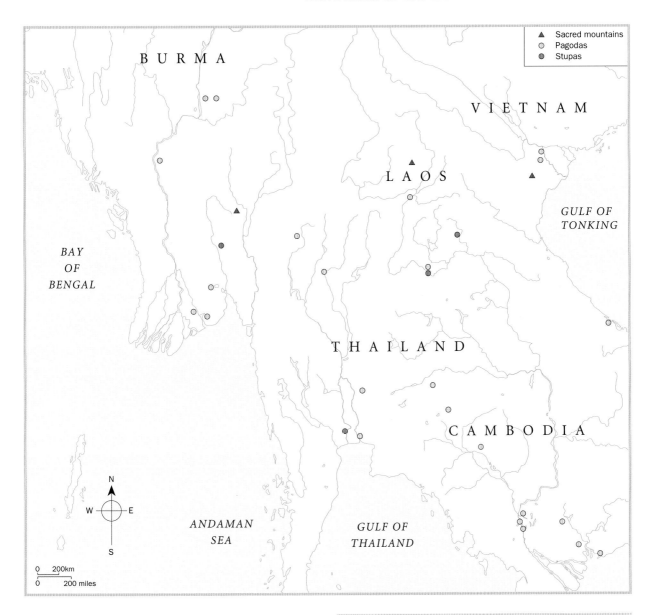

This map shows the location of sacred Buddhist sites in South-East Asia.

of Myanmar. But it was not until the founding of the kingdom of Ayutthaya in 1350 that Buddhism became the state religion with the king as head of the *sangha*. Later kings continued to protect, support and reform Buddhism. King Rama IV (ruled 1851–1868) spent 25 years as a monk before coming to the throne. He revised the sacred texts and founded a new order of monks. King Rama V (ruled 1868–1910) continued these policies and passed three 'Sangha Acts' to set out the duties of monks, particularly in the areas of healthcare and education.

MODERN THAI BUDDHISM

The close ties between the Thai king and the Buddhist sangha continue today. The king no longer has so much power but is still the honorary head of the *sangha*. Meanwhile, the government supervises the organization of the *sangha*. Buddhism remains very strong in Thailand, even as the country becomes more Westernized. Some 94 percent of the population are Buddhists. Many Thai men spend time in the *sangha* as part of their education. This has helped to strengthen the relationship betweeen lay Buddhists and the *sangha*.

CHAPTER 4: BUDDHISM IN CHINA, KOREA AND JAPAN

Buddhism reached China around the first century CE, probably spread by merchants travelling from India via Central Asia along the great trade route known as the Silk Road (see map). By the sixth century CE, Mahayana Buddhism had become one of China's main religions. From China, Buddhism spread to Korea and from there to Japan.

These stone sculptures are from the Longmen Caves, one of the most important Buddhist sites in China.

The arrival of Buddhism

When Buddhism first arrived in China, it was not a great success. The Chinese already had their own religious traditions – principally Confucianism and Taoism – and thought that these were superior to Buddhism. In spite of this, some Buddhist texts were translated into Chinese, and Chinese people began to join the *sangha*. By the fourth century CE, there were 24,000 Buddhist monks and almost 2,000 monasteries in China. Buddhism did not replace the Chinese religions but developed alongside them. The sixth to the ninth centuries CE were a golden age for Chinese Buddhism. Taoism remained popular with the aristocracy, but Buddhism appealed to ordinary people. During this period, many different schools of Chinese Mahayana Buddhism developed. In the ninth century, a backlash began against the power and wealth of the Buddhist monasteries. Buddhism survived but was greatly weakened. In the 12th century, it lost ground to Confucianism, which became the official state religion.

PILGRIM MONKS

To collect Buddhist texts for translation into Chinese, several Chinese monks made long, gruelling journeys to India. Fa-hsien (338–422 CE) set off in 399. He finally reached India after crossing the deadly Takla Makan Desert and the Pamir Mountains, which were said to shelter dragons that spat out poison. More than 200 years later, another monk, Hsuan-tsang (602–664) followed in Fa Hsien's footsteps. Hsuan Tsang visited many Buddhist sites in India, including Nalanda University (see page 17), and brought back so many texts that he needed 20 horses to carry them all.

Chinese Buddhist schools

Two of the most popular schools of Chinese Buddhism were Ching t'u (Pure Land) and Chan (Zen in Japanese). Pure Land is based on the worship of the Buddha Amitabha, who is believed to live in a heavenly land called the Pure Land. If people have faith in Amitabha and chant his name, they will be reborn in the Pure Land. From there they will be able to progress easily towards enlightenment.

Tradition says that Chan was brought to China by the Indian monk Bodhidharma in the early sixth century CE. It is a type of Buddhism based on meditation as a way of experiencing reality and seeing the world as it really is. Many different meditation techniques are used. One method is simply to sit quietly for long periods, with no thoughts or wishes, staring at a wall.

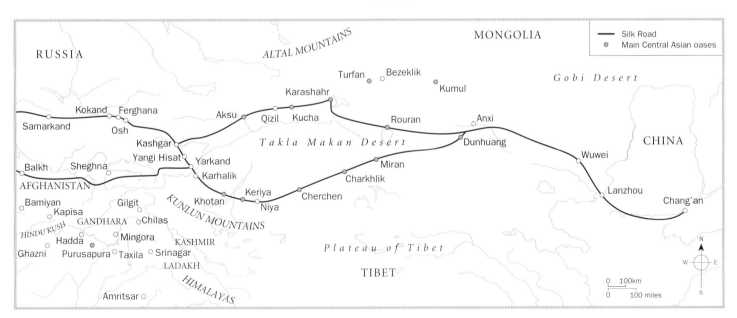

The Silk Road crossed Central Asia, linking China with India and the West.

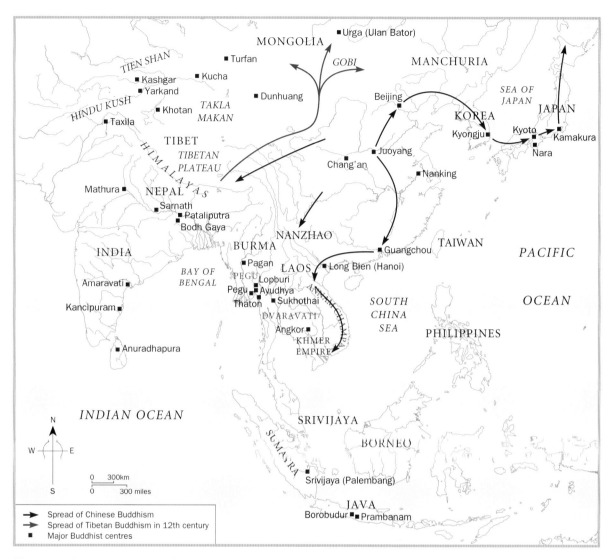

This map shows the spread of Buddhism to China, Japan and Korea.

Decline of Chinese Buddhism
In 1949, China came under Communist rule. The Communists harshly suppressed Buddhism and other religions. This persecution was particulary brutal during the Cultural Revolution (1966–1969) when Buddhism was practically wiped out. In the 1980s, some Buddhist temples were rebuilt and Buddhist organizations revived. This revival was halted in the late 1980s, however, when the Communist government cracked down on Buddhism again.

Buddhism reaches Korea
Even though Buddhism declined in China, Chinese Buddhism had a major influence on the rest of the region. Buddhism may have reached Korea in the fourth century CE when Chinese monks visited Korea. They brought Buddhist texts and images and built several monasteries. Buddhism flourished during the Silla Dynasty (618–935 CE) when it received royal support. Silla monks travelled to China and India to bring back the latest teachings. Buddhism remained the state religion until the 14th century.

The first ruler of the Koryo dynasty (918–1392) was King T'aejo, a devout Buddhist, who built ten great monasteries in his capital. Senior monks were appointed as royal advisors and it was usual for members of the royal family to become monks. A new edition of the Korean scriptures, running to over 5,000 volumes, was also collected and printed at this time. Under the Koryos, the monasteries became very rich and powerful.

Their powers were greatly reduced during the Choson dynasty (1392–1910), when stricter rules were drawn up for the monks. Even so, Buddhism continued to enjoy royal support for many years.

Modern Korean Buddhism

From 1910 to 1945, Korea came under Japanese control. Monasteries were divided up and there were conflicts between different groups of monks. The monk Han Yongun (1879–1944) campaigned hard during these years to protect Korean Buddhism. After World War II (1939–1945), the country was divided into North Korea and South Korea. The Communist government in the north stamped down on religion, and Buddhism was almost wiped out. In the south, Buddhism is still going strong. Many 'new religions' have been established in South Korea, most of which are new forms of Buddhism.

CHINUL AND CHOGYE

One of the most important Korean Buddhists was the monk Chinul (1158–1210). He became a Son (Chan) monk when he was seven years old. Chinul passed all his monastic examinations, but instead of rising to a high position in the *sangha*, he decided to form his own Buddhist school. It was called the Chogye school and attracted many followers, including the king. When Chinul opened his Suson Monastery in 1205, the king declared 120 days of national celebrations. Chogye remains the main Korean school, and the Suson Monastery continues to be a major centre of Korean Buddhism.

Colourful lanterns have been hung outside the Pulguk-sa Buddhist Temple in Kyongu, Korea.

Buddhism in Japan

Mahayana Buddhism came to Japan from Korea in the sixth century CE. A Korean king sent a mission to the Japanese emperor, which included Buddhist monks carrying texts and images of the Buddha. Under Prince Shotoku (ruled 574–622), Buddhism flourished in Japan, existing alongside Shinto, the ancient Japanese religion. Shotoku built Buddhist temples and monasteries and made Buddhism the state religion. In the eighth century, two forms of Chinese Buddhism – Tendai and Shingon – became popular. Both had mountain-top monasteries as their headquarters in Japan. In the 12th and 13th centuries, new schools developed, including Zen. Zen monasteries played an important role in protecting the teachings of Buddhism during the unsettled 14th and 15th centuries when many wars were fought between rival warlords. The 16th and 17th centuries saw the arrival of Christian missionaries in Japan. To preserve Buddhism, the emperor ordered all Japanese people, religious or not, to register with a Buddhist monastery.

A great teacher

One of the greatest teachers of Japanese Buddhism was the monk Nichiren (1222–1282). He trained at the great Tendai monastery on Mount Hiei outside Kyoto, but left to form his own school of Buddhism. He simplified the Tendai teachings to focus on the Lotus Sutra (see panel), and taught his followers that by simply chanting the name of the Lotus Sutra, they could purify their minds. Nichiren was frequently persecuted because of his outspoken attacks on other Buddhist groups. He escaped execution but was banished to a remote island. Despite this, Nichiren's influence remains strong to this day, and several modern Japanese Buddhist groups follow his teachings (see panel on page 29).

The great Buddha statue at Kamakura in Japan dates from the 13th century.

28

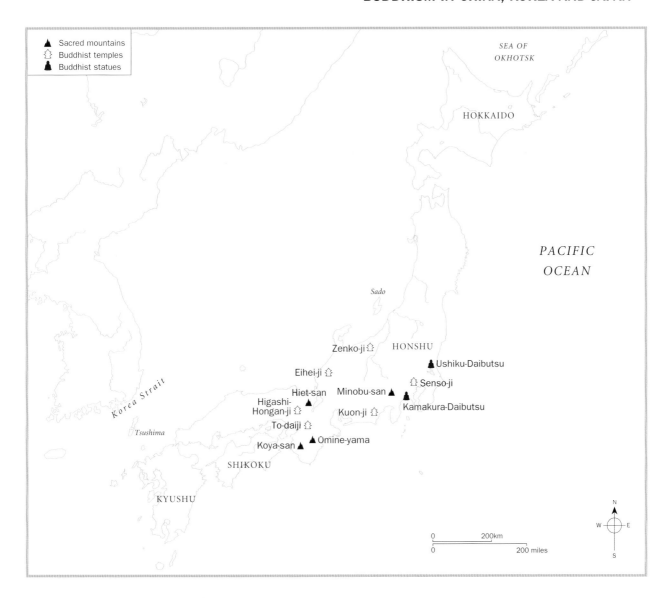

Key:
- ▲ Sacred mountains
- ⛩ Buddhist temples
- ▲ Buddhist statues

SEA OF
OKHOTSK

HOKKAIDO

PACIFIC
OCEAN

Sado

Zenko-ji ⛩   HONSHU

Eihei-ji ⛩   ▲ Ushiku-Daibutsu

Hiet-san ▲   Minobu-san ▲   ⛩ Senso-ji

Higashi-
Hongan-ji ⛩   Kuon-ji ⛩   Kamakura-Daibutsu

To-daiji ⛩

Koya-san ▲   ▲ Omine-yama

SHIKOKU

KYUSHU

Korea Strait

Tsushima

0   200km
0   200 miles

This map shows sacred Buddhist sites in Japan, including mountains, temples and statues.

THE LOTUS SUTRA

The Lotus Sutra is one of the most important and popular Mahayana Buddhist texts. It is treated with great honour and respect. A long collection of stories and verses, it takes the form of a talk given by the Buddha to a huge audience of followers and *bodhisattvas* (see page 11). One of its key teachings is that everyone, not simply holy men and women, can achieve enlightenment. To illustrate this, the Buddha compared himself to a raincloud that rains down on every plant equally. In the same way, the Buddha's teachings are available to everyone equally.

Modern Japanese Buddhism

In the 19th century, Shinto became the state religion of Japan and remained so until the end of World War II. But Buddhism continued to thrive. Today, about 75 percent of Japanese people regard themselves as Buddhists. Many actually follow a mixture of Buddhism and Shinto, and in many places Buddhist temples and Shinto shrines stand side by side. In addition, many new religious groups have sprung up. These are based on ancient Buddhist teachings but in a different form. They include Soka-gakkai, which is a form of Nichiren Buddhism.

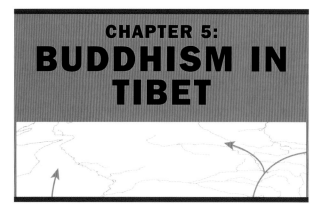

CHAPTER 5: BUDDHISM IN TIBET

Contact with India during the seventh century CE led to the introduction of Buddhism into Tibet. A long struggle followed between Buddhism and the local religion of Bon (see page 31). By the 14th century, however, Buddhism had become the state religion. For centuries, Tibet remained a Buddhist country with thriving monasteries and thousands of monks. Today, under Chinese rule, Buddhism faces an uncertain future (see page 35).

Early Tibetan Buddhism The story of Buddhism in Tibet begins with King Songsten Gampo (ruled c. 609–650 CE). Two of his wives, a Nepalese princess and a Chinese princess, were devout Buddhists. It is unclear whether the king himself converted to Buddhism, but he built two magnificent Buddhist temples, the Jokhang and the Rampoche, for his wives. These housed two statues of the Buddha that they had brought with them as dowries. A later king, Khrisong Detsen (ruled 755–797), made Buddhism the state religion with the help of great Indian teachers, including

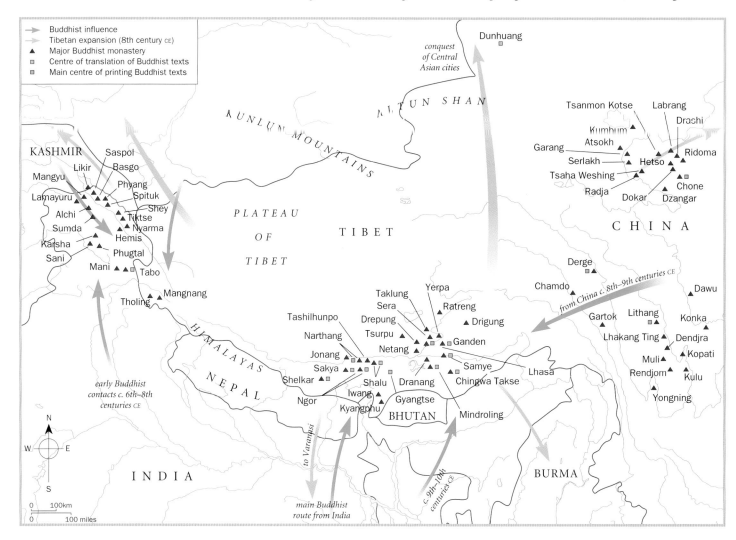

This map shows the growth of Buddhism in Tibet and other major Buddhist centres.

Padmasambhava (see panel). This did not occur without opposition, and a long struggle began between Buddhism and Bon, the established religion of Tibet at this time. King Ralpachan (ruled 817–836) went even further and became a Buddhist monk. He was assassinated by his brother, Langdarma, a strong supporter of Bon. Langdarma persecuted the Buddhists, destroying monasteries and killing many monks. In 842, however, he himself was killed by a Buddhist monk. In the 10th and 11th centuries, many monks fled to Tibet from India to escape the Muslim attacks. As a result, Tibetan Buddhism revived and flourished.

Translating texts King Songsten Gampo sent a translator to India to create an alphabet for the Tibetan language, which had not yet been written down. This enabled Buddhist sacred texts from India to be translated from Sanskrit into Tibetan. By the eighth century, Tibetan translators were hard at work, and over several centuries they created a huge collection of holy books. Tibetan texts are placed into two main groups – the Kanjur and the Tenjur. The Kanjur has 108 volumes and contains the words of the Buddha. The Tenjur has 360 volumes and contains commentaries on the Kanjur texts. This work also helped to preserve the original Indian texts, as Buddhism declined in India.

LOTUS BORN

In the late eighth century, the famous Indian teacher, Padmasambhava, arrived in Tibet. He helped establish Buddhism among the ordinary Tibetan people. Padmasambhava's name means 'lotus born', and legend says that he was born from a lotus flower. He was considered a great saint with amazing magical powers. According to tradition, King Khrisong Detsen organized a magic contest between Padmasambhava and the most powerful Bon priests and their demon allies. Padmasambhava is said to have used spectacular feats of magic to overcome them and convert them to Buddhism. During Padmasambhava's time, the first Buddhist monastery was built at Samye, and the first Tibetans became monks.

A Tibetan Buddhist monk reads the sacred texts.

Tibetan Buddhism

Tibetan Buddhism A unique form of Buddhism is practised in Tibet, known as tantric Buddhism. Tantric Buddhism is a type of Mahayana Buddhism that uses magic spells and rituals to help people gain enlightenment. It gets its name from a collection of mysterious sacred texts called the Tantras and was introduced into Tibet by Padmasambhava (see page 31). Tibetan Buddhism is sometimes called Vajrayana, which means 'thunderbolt' in Sanskrit. This is because it is seen as a particularly swift path to enlightenment, as fast as a speeding thunderbolt.

This image of the bodhisattva, Avalokitesvara. Tibetans believe that the Dalai Lama is Avalokitesvara in human form.

MARPA AND MILAREPA

The Kagyupa group within Tibetan Buddhism was founded by a great Buddhist teacher called Marpa (1012–1096). His disciple, Milarepa (1040–1123), became one of Tibet's most revered saints. Legend says he turned to Buddhism to make amends for using magic to punish his uncle. After his training with Marpa, Milarepa spent most of the rest of his life living in a lonely mountain cave. He dressed in rags and ate a diet of boiled nettles. Despite his harsh existence, Milarepa is famous for his collection of songs and poems, which tell of the joy of enlightenment. Known as *The Hundred Thousand Songs of Milarepa*, this remains one of the most popular sacred texts of Tibetan Buddhism.

Different schools From the ninth century, several different schools of Tibetan Buddhism developed. The oldest is the Nyingmapa group, which traces its teachings back to Padmasambhava. He is thought to have buried a collection of sacred texts in the mountains, ready for the time when people would be ready for their teachings. The Kadampa group was founded by another Indian monk, Atisha (982–1054). It stressed discipline and morality and had strict rules for its monks. Another group, the Sakyapas, were named after the grey colour of the earth around their monastery. They became very powerful in the 12th and 13th centuries.

The rise of the Gelukpas By the 13th century, Buddhism was flourishing in Tibet. Several of the Buddhist groups became involved in politics. In 1240, the Mongols from the north-west threatened to invade Tibet. To protect Tibet, the head of the Sakyapas, Sakya Pandita (1182–1251), travelled to the Mongol court. He offered to become spiritual advisor to the Mongol leader in return for Tibet being left in peace. The plan worked and the Sakyapas became the effective rulers of Tibet.

By the early 15th century, however, power had passed to another group. The Gelukpas were founded in 1409 by the Tibetan teacher Tsong-Kha-pa (1357–1419). He built the great monasteries of Ganden, Drepung and Sera for his followers. In their heyday, these monasteries were like small cities, housing tens of thousands of monks. In the 16th century, the leader of the Gelukpas was given the title Dalai Lama by the Mongols. The title means 'ocean of wisdom', meaning someone whose wisdom is as deep as the ocean.

This map shows the major Buddhist temples and monasteries of Tibet.

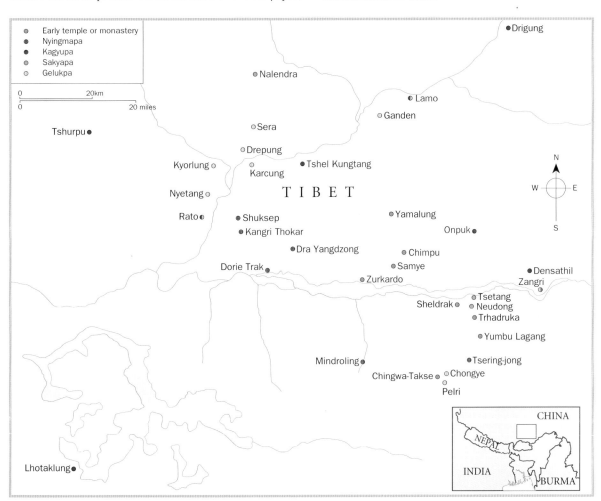

The Dalai Lamas The title of Dalai Lama was given to Sonam Gyatso (1543–1588) but he applied the honour to two previous Gelukpa leaders. Consequently, Gedun Truppa (1391–1475) is considered the first Dalai Lama. The current Dalai Lama is the 14th (see panel). Tibetans believe that the Dalai Lama is the incarnation of the *bodhisattva*, Avalokitesvara, who deliberately chose to be reborn in human form in order to help other suffering beings. When a Dalai Lama dies, a search is made for a baby who is his next incarnation. He is known by various signs; for example, he may be able to recognize old friends from his previous incarnation, or pick out belongings such as prayer beads. The baby is taken from his family and spends many years in Lhasa, the Tibetan capital, being educated.

By the 17th century, the fifth Dalai Lama (1617–1682) had become the religious and political leader of Tibet. He built the famous Potala Palace in Lhasa. Over the following centuries, the Dalai Lamas were caught up in political intrigue, particularly over Chinese claims to Tibet. During this time, the Dalai Lamas were forced to give up some political power to the Chinese. This remained the situation until the 13th Dalai Lama (1875–1933) assumed full power and ruled Tibet until his death.

Chinese invasion

In 1951, Chinese Communist forces invaded Tibet. At first, efforts were made to combine Communism with Buddhist religious freedom. But Communists objected to many Buddhist practices, and many Tibetans objected to Chinese rule. Thousands of monks were imprisoned or killed, and the teachings of Buddhism were outlawed. In 1959, after an unsuccessful Tibetan uprising, the 14th Dalai Lama was forced to flee from Lhasa in disguise. He settled in India where he was joined by some 100,000 fellow Tibetans. Those left behind suffered terribly. Worse was to follow during the Chinese Cultural

THE 14TH DALAI LAMA

The present Dalai Lama, Tenzin Gyatso (born 1935), is the 14th. He was taken to Lhasa at the age of five and made head of state at the age of 16. From his home in India, the Dalai Lama travels all over the world, campaigning for the rights of the Tibetan people. His warmth, wisdom and compassion have made him a much-loved and respected statesman. In 1989, he was awarded the Nobel Peace Prize for his work.

Tenzin Gyatso, the 14th Dalai Lama, at his home in Dharamsala, India.

Revolution of the 1960s. Buddhist temples and works of art were systematically destroyed, and the great monasteries were reduced to ghost towns. In the space of 20 years, a centuries-old way of life had been devastated.

Tibetan Buddhism in exile
Today, the Dalai Lama and his many Buddhist monks are still based in Dharamsala, India, where they have established a thriving Tibetan community and government in exile. The town has several Buddhist monasteries and temples, a school of Tibetan studies and workshops where traditional works of Tibetan Buddhist art are produced. Since 1980, the Chinese rulers have granted some limited religious freedom in Tibet, but the Dalai Lama has not been allowed to return, and Buddhism in Tibet faces a very uncertain future.

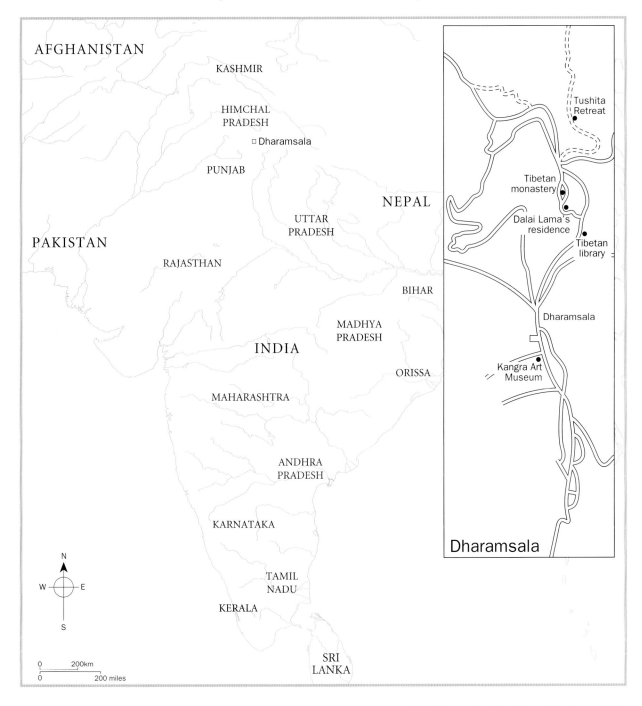

This map shows the location of Dharamsala in India where the current Dalai Lama has lived in exile since 1959.

CHAPTER 6:
BUDDHISM IN THE MODERN WORLD

Buddhism faces many challenges as it moves into the 21st century. In its traditional Asian homeland, the 20th century proved a time of mixed fortunes. In some countries, Buddhists faced persecution under brutal governments. In others, war and national unrest put Buddhism under threat. Recently, however, Buddhism has begun to re-establish itself in countries such as India and Indonesia. It is also gaining new followers in non-Asian countries, especially in Europe, North America and Australia.

Buddhism and society In Asian countries such as Thailand and Sri Lanka, Buddhism is still the main religion and has a very strong influence on society. For centuries, the *sangha* has played, and continues to play, a vital role. Monks are involved in education, health and social work, and in conservation. They continue to act as spiritual advisors to local communities, helping people to live according to Buddhist principles. In return they are treated with great respect by the local people, as they have been for hundreds of years.

Buddhist monks protest against an alcohol company in Bangkok, Thailand.

Engaged Buddhism Many Buddhists today, in Asia and beyond, are becoming involved in 'engaged Buddhism'. This means becoming involved, or engaged, in many aspects of social work, peace campaigning, politics and human rights. For example, Buddhists have set up hospitals and AIDS charities, become involved in prison visiting, and led protests against global concerns such as the international arms trade. One famous example of engaged Buddhism is the Wat Tham Krabok monastery in Thailand. For the last 50 years, the monks and nuns at this monastery have run a very strict but successful detoxification programme for drug addicts. The programme is based on Buddhist principles.

BUDDHISM IN INDIA

Although Hinduism and Islam are today the major religions of India, Buddhism has shown some signs of revival. This was largely through the work of Dr B. R. Ambedkar (1891–1956), an Indian lawyer and politician. He was born into a Dalit family, the lowest rank of Indian Hindu society. Hostility against his campaigns for equal rights for Dalits led Ambedkar to convert to Buddhism. Millions of other Dalits followed his example.

Theravada Buddhism
Mahayana Buddhism
Tibetan Buddhism

This map shows where different forms of Buddhism are practised in Asia today.

Buddhism and politics

In many Asian countries, Buddhism has suffered greatly under Communist and military regimes. Vietnam has been under Communist rule since the 1950s. But Buddhism has continued alongside Communism, although the *sangha* is regulated by the government. In Cambodia, however, Buddhism was practically wiped out. From 1975 to 1979, a Communist movement called the Khmer Rouge held power. Under its leader, Pol Pot, many monasteries were destroyed, and thousands of monks were tortured and killed. In 1979, a delegation of monks had to be sent from Vietnam to revive Cambodia's *sangha*. Today, Buddhism is officially the state religion of Cambodia, but its recovery is slow and its future still hangs in the balance.

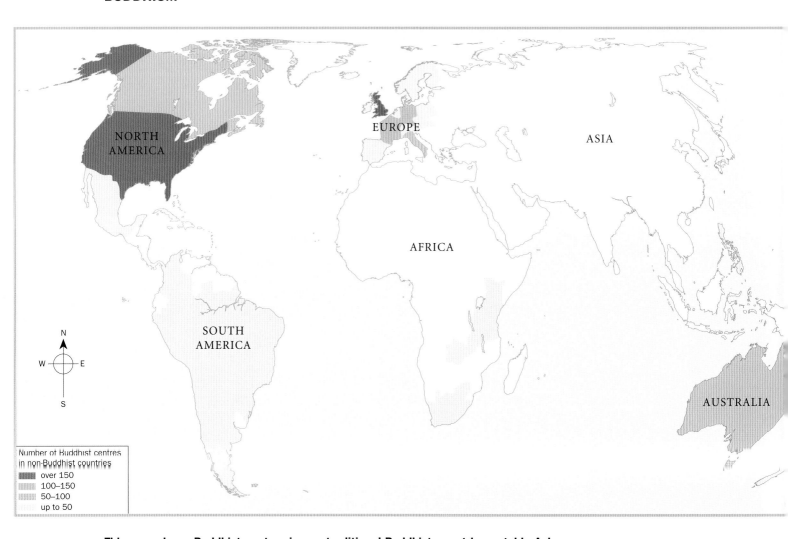

This map shows Buddhist centres in non-traditional Buddhist countries outside Asia.

Number of Buddhist centres
in non-Buddhist countries
- over 150
- 100–150
- 50–100
- up to 50

Buddhism in the West

Until about 100 years ago, very few people in the West had heard of Buddhism. But over the last century, there has been much greater contact between Buddhism and the West. Buddhism has grown rapidly and attracted thousands of followers. It has now become firmly established in Britain, the USA, Australia and in most European countries, and is becoming more popular in South America and Africa.

Buddhist scholars

The British made contact with Buddhism in the late 18th and early 19th century when the British Empire expanded to include Buddhist countries such as Myanmar and Sri Lanka. Some of the first Westerners to study Buddhism were British civil servants working in these countries. Other Buddhist countries, such as Vietnam and Cambodia, came under French rule and French scholars also began to study Buddhism.

In 1879, Edward Arnold, a British teacher in India, published a poem called 'The Light of Asia', which was based on the Buddha's life. This helped to spread an awareness of the Buddha, but serious scholarship really began in Britain in 1881 when the Pali Text Society was founded by British scholar T. W. Rhys Davids (1843–1922). He had first come across Buddhism when working for the British civil service in Sri Lanka. The society collected Theravada Buddhist texts and translated them, making Buddhism accessible to many more people in the West.

Buddhist societies

At the start of the 20th century, the first Westerners became Buddhist monks. Among them was a British man, Alan Bennett (1873–1923). He was ordained in Myanmar and took the Buddhist name Ananda Maitreya. He helped to found the first Buddhist society in Britain in 1908. In 1926, a Sri Lankan, Anagarika Dharmapala (1874–1933) founded a Buddhist centre in London, the first outside Asia. Buddhist societies were also formed in Germany (1903 and 1924) and France (1929). The Buddhist Society of America was formed in 1930 in New York City, USA.

Since then, interest in Buddhism has grown rapidly, and new centres and societies open every year. There are currently over 100 centres in Britain and many more in the USA. Some are mainly for people who have emigrated from Asia. Others mainly cater for Westerners who want to learn meditation or follow a Buddhist way of life. There are also many Buddhist monasteries, run by western monks and nuns.

Madame Helena Petrovna Blavatsky (1831–1891).

THE THEOSOPHICAL SOCIETY

Another organization called the Theosophical Society helped to introduce Buddhist ideas to the West. Founded in 1875 in New York by two Americans, Colonel Henry Steel Olcott (1832–1907) and Helena Blavatsky (1831–1891), it drew its ideas from many different ancient traditions, including Hinduism and Buddhism. Olcott and Blavatsky may have been the first Westerners formally to become Buddhists. On a visit to Sri Lanka in 1880, they visited a temple and pledged themselves to Buddhism in the presence of a Buddhist monk.

Western Buddhists take part in a Tibetan Buddhist ceremony in Dharamsala.

Buddhist traditions in the West

Before the 1950s, almost the only type of Buddhism known in the West was Theravada. A Sri Lankan *vihara* (Buddhist temple) was set up in London in 1954, followed by a Thai *vihara* in 1966. In the mid-1950s, Japanese Zen Buddhism also became popular in Britain and the USA. In the 1960s and 1970s, Tibetan refugees set up centres in the USA, Britain, Europe and Australia. A Tibetan monk called Chogyam Trungpa established the Samye Ling Monastery in Scotland, and a Tibetan Buddhist centre in the USA. It is estimated that, today, about half of Western Buddhists follow a form of Tibetan Buddhism. Other smaller groups have become well established, such as Japanese Pure Land and Shingon. Modern Buddhist groups have also grown up, including Soka-gakkai, a branch of Nichiren Buddhism (see page 28). Its teachings are based on daily chanting as a means not only to spiritual but also to material rewards. Many Buddhists have criticized its approach.

New Kadampa movement
One of the fastest-growing Buddhist groups in the West is the New Kadampa tradition. Founded by the Tibetan monk Geshe Kelsang Gyatso Rinpoche, it has over 900 meditation centres in 37 countries. New Kadampa is based on Kadampa Buddhism, which dates back to 11th-century Tibet (see page 33). It emphasizes moral discipline, study and meditation as ways to peace and happiness. Followers of New Kadampa also worship a spirit called Dorje Shugden. In 1998, the first New Kadampa temple was built in Cumbria, Britain. A second temple is nearly finished in New York City, USA, and further temples are planned.

FRIENDS OF THE WESTERN BUDDHIST ORDER

The Friends of the Western Buddhist Order (FWBO) was started in 1967 by an English Buddhist monk, Venerable Sangharakshita (born as Denis Lingwood). During World War II, he was stationed in India and Sri Lanka. He stayed on in Asia after the war and was ordained as a Theravada monk. He also studied the teachings of Tibetan and Chan Buddhism. He decided to form a Buddhist movement that combined elements of the traditions he had studied in a way that was suited to Western society. For example, the FWBO does not have monks and nuns. Highly committed Buddhists take serious vows and are ordained as 'members'. They do not wear robes but have a scarf, called a *kesa*, for special ceremonies.

Future of Buddhism In some traditionally Buddhist countries, such as Thailand and Sri Lanka, the original values and teachings of Buddhism – tolerance, compassion and morality, amongst others – have been undermined by a growing concern with material wealth. In other places, where Buddhism has arrived more recently, it is precisely these values that have attracted new followers. Even for people who are not religious, Buddhist ideas and practices, such as meditation, have been influential. But what lies in store for Buddhism? A key Buddhist teaching states that nothing stays the same for ever. Everything is always changing. By adapting to different cultures and circumstances, Buddhism has established itself as a major world faith and its future looks to be healthy and bright.

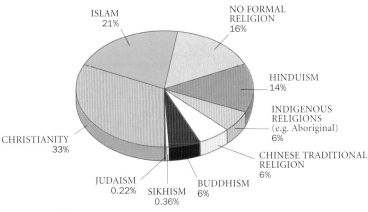

This pie chart shows the size of the world's Buddhist population compared to other faiths.

A map showing the places where different faiths are in the majority.

GREAT LIVES

Siddhartha Gautama (c. 563–483 BCE)

The son of an Indian nobleman, who became the Buddha. Siddhartha was born in Lumbini, Nepal, and lived a life of luxury in his father's palace. Having seen people suffer for the first time, he left this life behind to live as a monk, searching for the truth behind life. Having achieved enlightenment, he realized what caused people to suffer and spent the rest of his life teaching a way to end suffering and to live a better life.

Ashoka (ruled c. 265–238 BCE)

Ashoka was an Indian ruler of the Mauryan Empire who converted to Buddhism. He did much to promote Buddhist teachings by carving edicts on rocks and pillars placed around his empire. He also sent out many missionaries, including his own son and daughter, to spread the Buddha's teachings beyond India.

Asvaghosa (first century CE)

Asvaghosa was a poet at the court of the Kushan king Kanishka. He wrote many works on Buddhism in Sanskrit, including the first biography of the Buddha, entitled the *Buddhacarita* (Acts of the Buddha). Written in the style of an epic poem, parts of the original work still survive. There are also Tibetan and Chinese translations.

Nagarjuna (150–c. 250)

Nagarjuna was the founder of the Madhyamaka school of Buddhism and the greatest Buddhist philosopher. He was born into a Hindu family but became a Buddhist as a young man. It is said that he was presented with a collection of sacred texts by the king of the Nagas (mythical serpents with magical powers).

Bodhidharma (c. fifth century)

Bodhidharma was an Indian monk who travelled to China and became the founder of Chan (Zen) Buddhism. It is said that he spent nine years sitting still and meditating, then taught this method of meditation to his followers. According to tradition, he decided to return to India but died before he could do so.

Atisha (982–1054)

Atisha was an Indian monk and teacher who strongly influenced the development of Buddhism in Tibet. He is said to have studied Buddhism in Indonesia before becoming abbot of the Buddhist university of Vikramasila in India. He was invited to Tibet in 1042 by the king, where he guided the monks on the Buddha's teachings.

Dogen (1200–1253)

Dogen was the founder of the Soto Zen school in Japan and a major figure in Japanese Buddhism. Dogen was born into an aristocratic family, which fell on hard times. At the age of 13 he entered the great Tendai monastery at Mount Hiei. He devoted the rest of his life to training his followers in the teachings and practices of Zen.

Nichiren (1222–1282)

Nichiren was a Japanese monk who founded the Nichiren school of Buddhism. The son of a fisherman, he joined a Tendai monastery at the age of 12. For many years he travelled from temple to temple, searching for the teachings of 'true Buddhism'. He was exiled for his outspoken beliefs and narrowly avoided being executed.

Thich Nhat Hanh (born 1926)

Thich Nhat Hanh is a Vietnamese Zen master who was ordained at the age of 16. In the 1960s, during the Vietnam War, he worked hard to help war-torn communities and to campaign for peace. He continued his peace work after leaving Vietnam and founded Plum Village in France, where people from different faiths can attend retreats.

Tenzin Gyatso (born 1935)

The current Dalai Lama was born in north-eastern Tibet. He was taken to Lhasa and installed on the throne in 1940, aged five. At the age of 16, he became head of state. In 1959, the Dalai Lama was forced to flee to Dharamsala in India with many of his monks. He continued to travel and work tirelessly on behalf of the Tibetan people. He was awarded the Nobel Peace Prize in 1989.

FACTS AND FIGURES

Approximate numbers of Buddhists worldwide, by tradition (2004)

Mahayana	56%	c. 185,000,000
Theravada	38%	c. 124,000,000
Tibetan	6%	c. 20,000,000

The countries with the highest percentages of Buddhists (2004)

Thailand	95%
Cambodia	90%
Myanmar	88%
Bhutan	75%
Sri Lanka	70%
Tibet	65%
Laos	60%
Vietnam	55%
Japan	50%
Macau	45%
Taiwan	43%

The countries with the largest Buddhist populations (2004)

China	102,000,000
Thailand	55,480,000
Vietnam	49,690,000
Myanmar	41,610,000
Sri Lanka	12,540,000
South Korea	10,920,000
Taiwan	9,150,000
Cambodia	9,130,000
Japan	8,965,000

Source: Buddha Dharma Education Association and BuddhaNet

Calendar of festivals

Month of festival	Event	What happens
April	Hana-Matsuri (Japanese Mahayana)	A flower festival marking the Buddha's birthday and the coming of spring in Japan.
April/May	Wesak (Theravada)	Special prayers are said and gifts are exchanged to mark the Buddha's birthday, enlightenment and passing.
June/July	Chokhor (Vajrayana)	A Tibetan and Nepalese summer festival marking the Buddha's first teaching of the Four Noble Truths.
June/July	Poson (Theravada)	A Sri Lankan festival marking the arrival of Buddhism on the island with huge street parades telling the story.
July/August	O-bon (Japanese Mahayana)	A time for remembering people who have died with feasts and folk dances.
July/August	Asala (Theravada)	A festival marked in Kandy, Sri Lanka, by a spectacular parade in which an elephant carries a sacred relic of a tooth said to have been the Buddha's.
August	Festival of Hungry Ghosts (Chinese Mahayana)	A time for remembering the story of one of the Buddha's followers who saved his mother from hell by offering a feast to all the monks.
October/November	Kathina (Theravada)	A time when lay Buddhists visit the temple to give gifts of new robes to the monks.
November	Loi Kratong (Theravada)	The festival of lights in Thailand at which people float lighted candles in the rivers and remember the Buddha's generosity and kindness.
November	Sangha Day (FWBO)	A festival that celebrates the love and friendship shared by the *sangha*. A special prayer is said and people renew their commitment to Buddhism.
February	Losar (Vajrayana)	The Tibetan New Year festival, when the prayer flags fluttering from the temples are taken down and replaced.

TIMELINE

BCE

c. 563	Siddhartha Gautama is born in Lumbini, Nepal.
c. 483	The Buddha passes away in Kushinagara, India.
c. 482	The First Council is held at Rajagrha.
c. 373	The Second Council is held at Vesali.
326	The armies of Alexander the Great reach India.
265–232	Reign of Emperor Ashoka
c. 250	Buddhism is introduced into Sri Lanka.
250	The Third Council is held at Pataliputra
155–130	Reign of King Milinda (Menandros).
first century	The Tipitaka is written down for the first time.

CE

first century	The first images of the Buddha are made in Gandhara; Buddhism reaches China and becomes established in Indonesia.
100	The Fourth Council is held in Kashmir.
fourth century	Buddhism probably reaches Korea.
fifth century	The University of Nalanda is at its height; Buddhism becomes established in Myanmar.
sixth century	Buddhism becomes established in Vietnam; Buddhism reaches Japan from Korea.
seventh century	Buddhism is introduced into Tibet.
c. 800	Borobodur is built on Java.
12th century	Buddhism becomes the religion of Cambodia; Buddhism almost disppears from India; Nalanda is destroyed by the Muslims.
1350	Buddhism becomes the religion of Thailand.
1391–1475	The first Dalai Lama in Tibet.
1881	The Pali Text Society is founded.
1908	The first Buddhist Society in Britain.
1930	The first Buddhist Society in the USA.
1935	Birth of the 14th Dalai Lama.
1956	In India, Dr Ambedkar converts many people to Buddhism just before his death.
1959	The Dalai Lama flees from Tibet.
1967	The FWBO is founded.
1989	The Dalai Lama wins the Nobel Peace Prize.

GLOSSARY

alms Charitable donations of food and other items to Buddhist monks and nuns.

arahats Theravada Buddhists who have gained enlightenment and are treated with great respect and reverence.

bodhisattvas In Mahayana Buddhism, mythical beings who have gained enlightenment and could become Buddhas, but choose to help other people overcome suffering.

bodhi tree The fig tree under which the Buddha is said to have gained enlightenment.

Bon The ancient religion of Tibet before Buddhism arrived. It involves the worship of many spirits, gods and demons. Bon priests use magic and sacrifices to keep the spirits happy.

Buddhism The religion based on the teachings of Siddhartha Gautama, who became the Buddha. These teachings are known as the Dharma.

Communist A system of government in which the state owns industries and businesses and abolishes different classes of society.

Confucianism An ancient Chinese religion founded by Confucius in the sixth century BCE. It teaches respect for other people and believes in honouring the memory of ancestors.

cremated When a dead body is burned to ashes.

dowry Goods or a sum of money traditionally given to an Indian bridegroom's family by a bride's family before a marriage.

edicts Orders proclaimed by a king or other authority.

enlightenment Achieving a state of spiritual understanding.

Hinduism The ancient religion of India, which began more than 4,000 years ago. Today, it is India's major religion with some 800 million followers.

incarnation An appearance of a god or god-like being in human form. For example, Tibetans believe that the Dalai Lama is an incarnation of the *bodhisattva* Avalokitesvara.

Islam A religion that began in the Middle East in the seventh century, based on the teachings of the Prophet Muhammad.

laypeople People who follow a religion but have not become monks or nuns.

Mahayana One of the two main branches of Buddhism. Mahayana means 'the great way'.

meditate Still or quieten the mind in order to experience inner peace. Meditation is a central part of Buddhist practice.

missionaries People who set out to teach people about a religion and convert them to that faith.

Muslims Followers of the religion of Islam.

nationalism Great loyalty or devotion to one's country.

nirvana The perfect peace and happiness entered when the cycle of birth and rebirth is broken and suffering ends.

ordained Describing a person who has undergone a special ceremony to become a monk, nun or member of a religious order.

patron A person who gives support to a particular cause.

pilgrimages Journeys made to places that are sacred to a religion.

relics Parts of a holy person's body or belongings, which are kept after his or her death as an object of reverence.

sangha The community of Buddhists. For some Buddhists, the *sangha* particularly means monks and nuns. For others, it includes laypeople as well.

Sanskrit An ancient Indian language used to write down many of the Mahayana sacred texts. It is also the sacred language of Hinduism.

Shinto The ancient religion of Japan. Its followers believe in spirits called kami, which live in animals, plants and natural places such as rivers and mountains.

stupas Dome-shaped Buddhist monuments originally built to house the Buddha's relics.

Taoism An ancient Chinese religion founded by Lao-tzu in the sixth century BCE. It teaches about the Tao or 'Way', the underlying spiritual force of the universe.

Theravada One of the two main branches of Buddhism. Theravada means 'the way of the elders'.

Tipitaka The sacred texts of the Theravada Buddhists.

vihara A Buddhist monastery or temple.

FURTHER INFORMATION

Books for younger readers

Puja: the FWBO book of Buddhist Devotional Texts (Windhorse Publications, 1999)

21st Century Religions: Buddhism by Anita Ganeri (Hodder Wayland, 2005)

World of Beliefs: Buddhism by Anita Ganeri (McGraw-Hill Children's Publishing, 2001)

Books for older readers

Buddhism: A History by Noble Ross Reat (Jain Publishing, 1994)

Buddhism and Politics in 20th-century Asia edited by Ian Harris (Continuum Publishing, 1999)

A Penguin Life: Buddha by Karen Armstrong (Penguin Books, 2001)

Websites

www.buddhanet.net
A Buddhist network giving information on a wide range of Buddhist topics.

www.fwbo.org
The official website of the Friends of the Western Buddhist Order.

www.newyorkbuddhist.org
The website of the New York Theravada *vihara*.

www.tibet.com
The official website of the Tibetan government in exile, with information about Tibetan Buddhism, language and art.

INDEX